15 Ways to Stay Alive

Daphne Gottlieb

Manic D Press
San Francisco

For you.
I did it all for you.

Grateful thanks are given to the publications in which some of these poems first appeared: *Eleven Eleven, Life as We Show It, McSweeney's Internet Tendency, The Nervous Breakdown, The Rumpus, Smart Tart Zine, sPARKLE and bLINK, Velvet Park,* and *The Walrus.*

There should be many, many more than 15 ways to thank all the people who have helped with this book: Crazy crazy love for all the flashbang to The San Francisco Liberation Front and The Thursday Six writing groups. Thanks to Cindy Emch, Dani Montgomery, MG Roberts and Abigail Wick for the feathers and wrenches on an early draft. Most biggest gratitude to Regina Marler and Rachel McKibbens for the extra matte finish. And thanks to Paul Dalton for shaking my chair. Some words fell out.

Author photo: Joie Rey Cohen

Library of Congress Cataloging-in-Publication Data

Gottlieb, Daphne, 1968-
15 ways to stay alive / Daphne Gottlieb.
    p. cm.
ISBN 978-1-933149-52-3 (pbk. original)
I. Title.
PS3557.O829A615 2011
811'.54--dc22

                         2011003926

CONTENTS

endnotes

reading daphne gottlieb: an introduction

Daphne Gottlieb's poetry insists on truth telling. Her work refuses boundaries; linguistic and cultural pyrotechnics smash through pre-conceived notions of contemporary poetics. These poems formally and thematically traverse barriers of aesthetic, poetic, and political division to spark new and incendiary meanings. The inclusion of "external" narratives—of linguistic bits, of colloquial language, of pieces from the popular and mainstream press, of famous and found words across canonical and genre lines—has a long history, particularly since modernism. Gottlieb's poems are informed by and make their own place in this tradition.

In their "sampling" of other texts and their recontextualization of voices, these poems draw generatively on images and references whose meanings are amplified or transformed by their poetic re-sourcing. The contrapuntal mash-up of, for example, St. Augustine and a BDSM manual, of Charles Bukowski and Kanye West, is made more meaningful by the location of the source material at the book's end rather than on the page itself. This location allows us to avoid oversimplified readings and reveals connections and disjunctions that are part of the new textured voice of the poem and that lay bare something about the myths under which we live.

Gottlieb's poems engage in a call and response with Adorno's famous claim that "to write poetry after Auschwitz is barbaric." *15 Ways to Stay Alive* questions speech value, narration, and access, asking critical questions of itself and poetics and politics in general: What is voice? What voices are heard and for what and by whom? Are any voices non-complicit? If not, then what? There is still the screaming. Can a book be a grenade? An activist space? Can a poem? What the book finally asserts is the popping power of the words on the page as words, as frame, as highly or hypertextual/textured language which refuses to be evacuated of meaning, and which in fact shimmers and shakes and reverberates with powerful claims about meaning and the requirement of language to create change.

Kirsten T. Saxton
Mills College

*"Unbeing dead
isn't being alive."
— ee cummings*

adage

Don't borrow
spilled milk.

Beggars don't have another
shoe to drop.

The pot's calling
the early bird.

Don't count
your chickens before

pigs fly, before pearls.
Don't call the sow's ear.

Clothes make
others. A rolling boy

gathers. One man washes
another. Unto. Others.

Take the boy
out of the country. Kill

two birds. Save nine. Walk
a mile. Unto. It is better

to give. It is better to grieve.
It is better to grift.

Receive. The hand
that feeds you

must come down.
The bite is worse.

God only gives you
a stitch in the side.

Kill two. Save nine.
Bless the sow purse,

the silk ear.
Make hay. Shine.

open water

There's a shark in Australia.
I live in San Francisco.
Today is Monday.
I am almost out of nicotine patches
and there are so many ways to be white
and all of them are wrong.

On the bus today, this woman
was telling me that doctors
cut off her antenna.
She sleeps much better now
but it's easier to sneak up on her.

Somewhere in Australia,
there is a shark swimming in
the open sea. I visit that shark
in my head
when things are bad.
The shark doesn't care.

I didn't go to a party last night
but I think I will go to one tonight
maybe.
You have to be careful
who you turn your back on.

I can't go to a party
with no one
to watch
my back. Here is what I
learned today on the TV: Now we have
healthcare. A shark can bite
another shark in half.
The important men are using
bad words at each other.
There are too many parties
not to go to.

Sharks do not sleep.
Now we have healthcare.
Some days I am the only
sane person in the world
and I get lonely.

On the bus, this woman was telling me
about the bullets in her vagina.

Not the same woman.
A different one.
I didn't tell her about my shark.

My friend's cat is sick.
He is now a five thousand dollar cat.
It is a five thousand dollar love.
It is a big love.
It is spring.

I am a girl
and there is also a boy.
It is more fun to think about boys
than sharks. The shark swims in small circles
at night when I am awake
and I am thinking about the boy.
Sharks do not sleep.

The shark thinks about food.
I worry about who has my back.
I worry about spring ending,
about the price of things.

There's a five thousand dollar love
in the belly of that shark.

lonely indonesia[1]

1. Checking In

I'd like a room.
Can I see the room?
Is there any better room?
I will take this room.

2. During Your Stay

Where can I wash my clothes?
Please wash these clothes for me.
When will they be ready?
Can I use the telephone?
Please spray my room.
There are mosquitoes in it.
Please change my sheets.
My room needs to be cleaned.

3. Complaints

Excuse me, I've got a problem here.
I can't open the door/window.
The toilet won't flush.
Can you get it fixed?
The room smells.
It's too dark.
It's too noisy.

4. At the Restaurant

We would like a table for five, please.

I can't eat
...milk and cheese
...eggs
...meat
...prawns.

This isn't cooked.
Not too spicy please.
No MSG please.
This is delicious.

5. Some Useful Phrases

How much is this?
Do you accept credit cards?
Do you have others?
Can I see it?
I don't like it.
I will take it.

6. Emergencies

I am ill.
I am lost.

Where is the police station?
Where are the toilets?

Could you help me please?
Could I please use the telephone?
I speak English.
I have medical insurance.

I don't understand.
I didn't realize that I was doing anything wrong.
I didn't do it.
I'm sorry. I apologize.

at the punk lit reading

There is a poet onstage.
He used to sort of stalk me.
I clapped at his poem
because it was over.
It was about heroin
or ripping someone off
or being in a band
or dead bodies.
Doesn't everybody want
to make a statement?

I'm too bored to burn
down the forest. See the trees?
Let's bang our heads
against them until

we see stars. The boy
next to me is cute.
When I kiss him
he tastes like the violent
deaths of vegetables.
Carrot blood. Banana bones.
He is unnerved.
He keeps ending up
in my poems. "Stop sitting
next to me, then," I say.
He says, "No."

The poet onstage just said,
"Raise your right hand
if you are dead." I can't
do that. I am writing
on napkins. Now a famous
punk rock girl is on stage.
She just said, "This is something
I kind of just made up today. It's kind of
like a poem. It's called 'Eliminating
the Blank.'" That's what I'm doing here.
It's something I kind of just made
up today. It's kind of like
a poem. I'm eliminating
the blank.

what you eat

Cats eat fish. Cats eat rats. There are
210 calories in a Snickers bar. There are
214 calories in an average rat. They say
the Donner Party didn't eat each other
after all. The bones they found belonged
to animals. Crime rates are higher
where there are slaughterhouses.
Do not confuse the abattoir with
the boudoir. Animals died to be oil
where they spilled back into the ground.
We are animal. 17.3 million Americans
went to bed hungry this year. An average cat
weighs 10 pounds. Bananas, Rice,
Applesauce, Toast. A 10-pound turkey
feeds 8 to 10 people. In sheer numbers,
the Native American genocide
exceeds the Holocaust. Depression,
withdrawal, anxiety, and trouble sleeping
are symptoms of Mad Cow Disease. Anthrax
is caused by cows and terrorists. There is evidence
that vegetables sense pain. There is
evidence that vegetables scream. Frogs' legs
taste like chicken. Chicken tastes like
chicken. A can of Chicken of the Sea
costs $1.89. 130,000 dolphins were killed
last year to make tuna. There is no nice
word for buffalo and chicken and rat,
but there is pork and beef and veal.
Say *abattoir*, not *slaughterhouse*.
If you die, a dog will wait a week
before eating your corpse. A cat
will wait a day.

pack animals

this morning I heard the cops
talking about teen runaways.
these kids have dogs, they said,
and the best way to deal with
this teen homeless problem,
they said, was to tell the kids
they were going to be in trouble
for having unlicensed dogs.
yeah, they said, they clear right out of there
when you tell them you're gonna call
animal care and control to take their dog
away, and the taxpayers are happy,
the taxpayers know you can't keep a dog
on the street anyway, why, a dog needs
to be cared for, and these kids
can't do it, a dog needs food,
and these kids don't have it,
a dog needs love
and these kids

preoccupation

If he had been a farmer, he would've worn overalls. If he were a surgeon, he would have worn scrubs. If he were a utility repairman, he would have worn a jumpsuit. If he were a sailor, he would have worn a sailor suit. If he were a clown, he would have worn a clown suit. If he were a swimmer, he would have worn a swim suit. If he were a law, he would have worn a law suit. He was a business man. He had regrets.

like I stole it

I wear mostly black.
Cat burglars wear black
and anarchists wear
black. The difference

between cat burglars
and anarchists is burglars
are quiet. There are no memorable
burgling chants. You can't

use a bullhorn to lift
someone's watch
but it's okay to
leave fingerprints

on a demonstration.
Don't carry a sign
to a B&E job. Don't
squat the house you

rip off. People in foreign
films also wear black.
When I do my laundry,
it looks like the television

is turned off. Rent is theft.
People who wear black smoke,
except when they don't.
Ninjas wear black

and are quiet.
Ninjas jump through
windows but so do
anarchists. And cat

burglars. I used to smoke
but I quit. Johnny Cash
wore black. And Zorro.
And Dracula. I never

use bleach. Morticia wore
black. Theft is
not theft. Robin Hood
should've worn black.

Death wears a black
black robe. I quit
smoking. I wore protest
black to a funeral

and everyone knew.
I can't save the world
by yelling. I'm too old
to kick high. My laundry's

almost dry. I've got
my black gloves on.
I've got my hand
in your pocket.

"The world is such a dangerous place, a man is lucky to get out of it alive." — W.C. Fields

no poetry after auschwitz

said Adorno, but there are still
poems, in a mark of arrogance or hope,
maybe both.

This is not a poem
it is a rock
through a window—

it is a smash
and run—
it is a broken capitalism machine

150 miles
from Baghdad.
The television is on at the law firm.

There is no business as usual.
The building is surrounded by fences
and riot cops

who are fighting the crime
of free speech, free assembly.
Yesterday they dragged a woman by her hair.

Today, last night, three days ago,
the Anarchists covered their faces,
hid Molotov cocktails in the bushes.

On our way to the protest, my friend tells me,
I am not covering my face.
It seems it's one of the fundamental freedoms left.

I have a bandana in my pocket
just in case.
I am trying to find ways

to stem my own anger,
my body a grenade rolling in the street
teeth clenched, handing out flowers

stolen from the lobby of a law firm
to the motorists we delay, thanking them
for their patience

while the U.S. bombs
the fuck out of another country
it has already starved to death.

I am trying to find reasons not
to smash things. Last night an American soldier
threw three grenades into commanders' tents.

They say he acted out of "resentment."
I understand resentment
I am practicing nonviolence

I shove my hands in my pockets
to make sure
I don't pick up a rock

2.
one Two
Three FOUR
we are the people

A Little Bit Louder Now
Who Are Going
TO STOP THIS WAR

There are protesters in white
armed with saxophones, drums,
dance training

Show me what democracy looks like?
THIS IS WHAT DEMOCRACY
LOOKS LIKE

The protesters in white have forgotten
the difference between protest
and performance,

the difference between comrades
and audience.
They will make the evening news.

3.
In New York
Ground Zero kids tell me
the cop psy-op wagon broadcast:

"The march is now over.
Please leave the area
in an orderly fashion."

New York stood in front of the truck,
got a bullhorn
and started shouting

"THE WAR IS NOW OVER.
PLEASE LEAVE IRAQ
IN AN ORDERLY FASHION."

In Chicago,
they are dancing in the streets
to block traffic.

This resistance
will not be joyless.
Outside the Federal Building,

a mobile generator
on a bike-drawn cart,
huge speakers

blare NOT IN MY NAME
a marching band plays "War Pigs"
the DJ's fist is in the air

a Dixieland band plays
"Down by the Riverside"
and we dance in the street

4.
Yes, remember
Rachel Corrie
killed by a bulldozer

but she put her own body
on the line
using her own privilege,

her own choice. How many
have died with nothing
but their borders to blame?

How many names will we never
hear because they
had brown skin, not white?

Because of lines they
never drew and could not
get outside of? Because

they
are not
"ours"?

5.
Whose streets?
OUR STREETS.
Whose streets?

6.
The rich restaurateur who is
a San Francisco Supervisor
tells the news,

"We will prosecute
protestors to the fullest
extent of the law." Write

the Legal Aid phone number
on your forearm. Listen
for the order to disperse.

Go limp.
Do not fight the cops.
Watch your back.

7.
It is terrifying how quickly
"Free Palestine"
becomes

"End the Occupation"
becomes
"Kill the Jews"

8.
At work, the secretaries
are watching with shock and awe.
I want to know

if there's a body count.
12, they tell me.
Iraqis? Really?

Oh no, they say, sipping coffee,
eating salads, fries.
That's Americans.

That's the only number
we've heard.
That's the only number.

9.
Whose streets?
OUR STREETS!
Whose streets?

Thursday, we shut down the Federal Building.
We shut down Bechtel. We blitzed Halliburton.
We shut down the Bay Bridge.

I say "we" because I watched it on TV.
I say "we" because I was there.
I say "we" as I write this in sunny San Francisco

on a fully loaded computer
smoking multinational corporate cigarettes,
before I eat breakfast,
after I've slept adequately
in a warm house
full of love.

I am waiting for
text messages from the antiwar bloc
to show up on my cell phone.

10.
Lighting candles, signing petitions
blocking intersections, chanting,
walking until my feet are blistered

shouting until my throat is raw
I'm trying so hard to change things
but I can't even get the blood off my hands.

what it means to be young in new orleans[2]

starving there   (You have to be careful or you could start a riot just
                    giving away a bottle of water)
sitting around the bars
                    1 oz. Light Rum
                    1 oz. Dark Rum
                    1/2 oz. Passion Fruit Juice
                    1/2 oz. Lime Juice
and at night walking the streets for hours,
                    raped for hours until she was dead
the moonlight always seemed fake
to me, maybe it was,
                    under a 25-foot wall of water as Katrina
                    slammed the Gulf Coast
and in the French Quarter I watched
                    a 25-foot wall of water
                    rescue boats... bypassing the dead
the horses and buggies going by,
everybody sitting high
                    in hip-deep water, only to stand at the intersection,
                    on the neutral ground
in the open
                    you had to stand in other people's shit
in the open
                    School bus commandeered by renegade
in the open
carriages, the black
                    School bus
driver
                    renegade
and in
back the man and the woman,
                    Watching bodies float by
                    as they tried to escape the drowning city.
                    Picking up people along the way.
usually young and always white.
                    You see a black family, it says, "They're looting."
and I was always white.
                    You see a white family, it says, "They're looking for food."
and hardly charmed by
                    George Bush...
the world.
                    doesn't care about black people.

New Orleans was a place to
                    French Quarter stroll
                    ask for a go cup
                    Dixieland Jazz and live music
New Orleans was a place to
hide.
I could piss away my life,
unmolested
                    I don't want to see anymore goddamn press conferences
except for the rats
                    pick at unguarded corpses
the rats
                    host fleas, which can transmit typhus, typhoid fever,
                    plague, and other diseases
the rats
in my small dark room
                    endanger public health wherever
                    they mingle with people
very much resented sharing it
with me.
                    Some of the very sick became distressed.
they were large and fearless
and stared at me
                    If the first dose was not enough,
with eyes
that spoke
an unblinking
death.
                    I gave a double dose.
women were beyond me.
                    I injected morphine into those patients who were dying
                    and in agony.
they saw something
depraved.
                    And at night I prayed to God to have mercy on my soul.
there was one waitress
                    refused entry
a little older than
I, she rather smiled,
lingered when she
brought my
                    clean water
coffee.
that was plenty for
me, that was
enough.

there was something about
                  martial law
that city, though:
it didn't let me feel guilty
                  This is New Orleans, post-Katrina, and I love it.
that I had no feeling for the
                  ungodly quantities of food and drink,
                  ice, coolers, bikes, a couple scooters, candles,
that I had no feeling for the
                  flashlights, water, batteries, charcoal,
                  antibacterial hand wipes—
things so many others
needed.
                  All the more liquor for the rest of us
it let me alone.
                  This is New Orleans, post-Katrina, and I love it.
sitting up in my bed
                  the Pinot Grigio is chilling in the pool
the lights out,
                  electricity is a rumor
hearing the outside
sounds,
lifting my cheap
bottle of wine,
                  the Pinot Grigio is chilling in the pool
letting the warmth of
the grape
enter
me
                  a Miami Herald reporter sleeps in his own vomit.
as I heard the rats
moving about the
room,

I preferred them
to
humans.
being lost,
                  under federal control
being crazy maybe
                  under Bush
is not so bad
if you can be
that way:
                  privileged
undisturbed.

New Orleans gave me
          "shoot to kill" orders
          Displacement based on race
          Destruction of a people's culture
New Orleans gave me
that.
nobody ever called
my name.
no telephone,
no car,
no job,
     no what it means
no anything
        I'm not wrong... this feeling's gettin'
me and the
rats
and my
         forced evacuation
youth,
one time,
that time
I knew   what it means
even through the
nothingness,
it was
        Genocide
a
celebration
of something not to
do
of something not to
do   you know
of something not to
do   you know
but only
      know I'm not wrong
      the feeling's getting stronger
know   what it means to miss New Orleans?

to prove that I was someone[3]

Dare I take
My tattoo
the master-slave connection
my tattoo
a step further
is a rebel flag,
to point out
a rebel flag
to point out
roughly 3"x5"
that many people
on my lower back
many people
Having known people
of all races and ethnicities
that had enlisted in the military
have allowed themselves
enlisted in the military
to be
with tattoos
modern-day slaves
with tattoos

such as swastikas,
iron crosses, etc.
Indeed, a person does not
have to
etc. I though it wouldn't
be black
cause a problem.
to exhibit a slave mentality.
Apparently though, it has.
Unwittingly, too many of us—
The Army, the Air Force, and the
Marines
and it does not matter whether we
are black
the army
asian
the air force
chicano
and the marines
or white
have told me
or white
that any tattoo
we perpetuate "the Master's will"
considered racist or sexist
through our own self-hatred
will keep you from enlisting in the
military
and destructive behavior.

Is this some new policy
since 9/11?

For those individuals
who are in denial,

Is there anything I can do?

for those individuals
who are in denial,

I am 17 and have

here are some

recognizable signs of

a future ahead of me

self perpetuation of

slave behavior:

I have come from

be it

the bottom of society

in prison

and worked my entire life

in prison

to prove that I was someone

or

to prove that I was someone

in society

who was capable of status

in society

other than white trash.

Somebody please help me out.

so outrageous
(for Anna Nicole Smith and all the others)

1.   you tuned in. she's dead. you're sad. there's blood on your hands. you're worried it might stain.

2.   public redemption; recovery and could she be next did you share a surgeon a line a dream and a texas 12-step to excess, dance it for all the women, too loose, too loud, too raunchy, too greedy, too — always, we come back to this: death or stand down in sensible shoes? sit down shut up wear grey and don't move until you die. don't bleach a thing. you're too old now. keep doing it. we'll put it on film.

3.   enacting class rage laughing at her "marriage" or her "marriage," famous-for-nothing-she's-talentless rage, she's-a-trainwreck-do-you-BELIEVE/oh-no-she-didn't clucking, she's-so-fabulous, don't-you tsk-tsk watercooing. spare me, and spare me your grief now. rubberneck is ugly in all the february colors.

4.   i hope someone is taking care of your dog didn't i hear that you had a dog i hope your dog is okay you had a dog once upon a time you were 20 once upon a time you were four you sang songs with a knick-knack paddywhack you still know every hand part that goes with it

5.   did you ever wake up put your arms around the big can of trimspa, under satin duvet, dog sliding off yr pillow as yr weight shifts, the can in your arms before the first pill of the day and think yes. this is who i am. this is who i always wanted to

6.   die in a hotel

I've been understanding, but god told me there is something wrong[4]

5'10" I seem 5'8" I seem 6'2" I seem dead. Tall, confident. I am slender and strong, most say handsome, all say friendly, *I am single,* most say fit. Well endowed. Young, hung and eager to please.

155 lbs, 178 lbs, 210 lbs I am a good lover, I cook good meals. *Every evening I am alone. I go to bed alone.* I raised the kids. I am single. *Who knows why. I am not ugly or too weird.* I am single, most say fit. Well endowed.

No girlfriend since 1984, I had a healthy love life. I haven't even tried to meet anyone new. Most say handsome, all say friendly, all say *Another lonely night, I'm done. This is too much. Eighteen years.* No romance, no sex, no caring, no friendship. I miss love and sex.

What is it like to be dead? I just want to feel like I am wanted. *I always think I am forgetting something.* One time or more. I know this is a long shot. My lips would be sealed. Respectful and discreet. I am single. *I think I am always forgetting something, Similar to when you get in your car. You hesitate. A thought: "what am I forgetting?"*

Similar to when you get in your car: I have extra money and enjoy traveling, *too,* through Brazil, Uruguay, Argentina, Chile, Bolivia, Peru, Ecuador, Thailand, Malaysia, Indonesia, China, Pakistan, India, and Nepal. *LA was the best! But going alone is not too fun.* I entered a continent, wandered around. Moved on. *Going alone is not too fun.* I can't trust anymore. I do miss being with someone. It hurts.

You know how deadly it is, when they just don't understand. *Flying solo is a destroyer.* They just don't understand. You have that sinking feeling. They never will. You know how deadly it is.

nothing is as dirty as money[5]
(sandy and jessica explain the subprime mortgage crisis)

In an effort to make more money, I walked past Sandy's bedroom door. I heard banks relaxing their lending standards in the room. Putting my ear to the door, I listened in, hearing the increased demand for mortgages. I figured Sandy was masturbating, so slowly I opened the door, squeezing in as quietly as I could.

I peeked at the bed and I couldn't believe my luck. The blonde hair of Jessica was between Sandy's legs. To get more money to lend, Sandy and Jessica packaged mortgages together. Jessica's ass was positioned well to enter her from behind. "Oh yes, that's the way, lick me until I'm a 'security' for investment banks to buy," she said. Sandy's skirt was hiked up. This increased the amount of money available for lending and caused another round of standards relaxation. Jessica's standards were so relaxed, her shirt was pulled up above her breasts and she was playing with her nipples.

Jessica's tight white panties stretched across her ass. A wet spot was visible from where I was standing. I crept over to her, like the unaware and greedy consumers who took advantage of the relaxed lending standards. I pushed her skirt up further and pulled aside her panties to see her perfect pink pussy, shaved and smooth. She tried to look back but Sandy pushed her head back down to her pussy. "Those greedy customers borrowed more than they could afford," said Sandy, panting.

Jessica's pussy glistened with her woman juices because she couldn't afford the mortgages. Jessica gasped as my finger slid into her. "I'm going into default," she moaned. "I'm going into default!"

I knew it was time to foreclose on Sandy. She'd been quietly moaning, but she began to scream, "oh fuck, oh fuck, oh fuck, fuck, fuck." Jessica's tongue was working Sandy's clit now, and you could tell she was really suffering from the pricing. She screamed and panted as she came over my fingers. She sighed, sticky with the mess from borrowing and lending.

*"I think that just being alive
is so much work at something
you don't always want to do.
The machinery is always going.
Even when you sleep."*
— Andy Warhol

the unauthorized autobiography of black beauty[6]

Chapter 1: My Early Home

For my birthday, I told my mommy and daddy I wanted a pony.

Chapter 2: The Hunt

We're
on a
carousel   A crazy   Again
              carousel   we go
                           around   And now   We're   And up
                                       we spin   high   around
                                       around   above   again
                                                    the
                                                    ground

Chapter 3: My Breaking In

Line up the ponies
along a pink-ribbon starting line   when the music starts

the ponies must prance to the

                                       finish line

Chapter 4: Birtwick Park

There were six young colts in the meadow besides me. They were older
than I was; some were nearly as large as grown-up horses. I used to run
with them, and have great fun.

Chapter 5: A Horse Fair

It's Mister Ed's birthday and
he wants   The whole world
Wilbur to give him a party   madly turning
                                                              turning
Ed decides to take matters   turning
into his own hooves

Chapter 6: Till You Can't See

Little   girls   won't   be   able   to
resist   the charm   of   this   birthday   celebration.
The   Props   and   decorations are   sparkly,
the games   are sweet   and   inviting   and the   cake
and   Lemonade   are   deliciously
                                     pink.

Chapter 7: Trojans

It should come as no surprise
that the principle of the gift,

which propels
the movement

(the whole world madly
turning turning)

of general activity,
(quickly turning

for you and me)
is at the basis of sexual activity.

Chapter 8: The Pony

For my birthday, I told my mommy and daddy I wanted a pony.

Chapter 9: A Stormy Day

Interviewer:	Ponyboy:
We're	kind of small for fourteen
on a carousel	even though I have a good build, and
a crazy carousel	those guys were bigger than me
and now we go around	I automatically hitched my thumbs
again we go around	in my jeans and slouched
and up again around	wondering if I could get away
	if I made a break for it.

Chapter 10: The Devil's Trademark

We used to gallop
all together round
and round the field as hard
as we could go.

Sometimes we had rather rough
play, for they
would frequently bite
and kick

as well as gallop
bareback.

Chapter 11: The Old Hostler

play the part
of the Pony

trotting around
the outside of the circle

using her wand
to lightly tap her friends
on the back, saying
"horse, horse, horse,
horse…"
as she goes

When she taps someone
and says "pony,"
that girl jumps up and
trots behind her
around the circle and
back to the empty space.

again

we
go

around

and then

we go

horses were clearly on my mind
I made a couple of statements
that might get my parents arrested.

back then they all laughed.

"I'm going to marry a horse,
and feed him alfalfa."

"I'm going to have a baby

and it might be a horse."

Chapter 12: The Fire

Interviewer: Who do you think played that game horsey?
Child: Ray and Miss Peggy.
Interviewer: Ray and Miss Peggy? Did Miss Peggy take her clothes off?
Child: Yeah.
Interviewer: I bet she looked funny, didn't she? Did she have big boobs?
Child: Yeah.
Interviewer: Yeah. And did they swing around?
Child: Yeah.

Chapter 13: Liberty

Assume for the purposes
of this discussion
a loaded magazine is in the weapon
A live cartridge is in the chamber

Ponyboy says, "You get tough like me
and you don't get hurt.
you look out for yourself
and nothin' can touch you.

Interviewer: How did Ray
              touch you?

Child: With his finger.

Interviewer: How many
              times did he
              hit the horse?

Child: I don't know.

Chapter 14: Mustang Sally

She lubed up a plastic butt plug attached to a real horsehair tail and slid it inside my ass, tying knots here and there to secure it in place.

Interviewer: How about a finger in your hole?

after we did it
I laid there
admiring her
while she
in

the first time
on the bed
beauty
tended to herself

in the sheets
there was a man
dancing

on a carousel
a pretty
carousel
and suddenly
we feel

while she tended

to herself

in the bathroom.

to the simple
rock & roll song

Chapter 15: The Rock & Roll Song

Angel looks down at him and says
"Oh, pretty boy,
can't you show me
nothing
but surrender?"

The hammer is fully cocked,
the safety lock is off,
the grip safety
is depressed
the trigger is squeezed
and the round is ignited.

Chapter 16: Pony Keg

You never know   what is going to happen   when there's a round of shots

Chapter 17: The Colt .45

Interviewer: Was the horse standing?
Child: Laying down.

Chapter 18: Merrylegs

Everyone seems to be riding Mister Ed and he's getting sick of it.
Tonight, the singer's a hoarse whisperer.

Chapter 19: A Talk in the Orchard

I still watch them each morning   Yes, he is small
        on my drive to work—   but he is quick and willing
      impossibly long-legged   and kind-hearted, too
      beautiful though coltish   and then he wishes
   hair shimmering over tawny   very much to come
                    muscles   and his father would like it
    as they make their way to   said I was quite agreeable
                  tomorrow
these yearling Thoroughbred fillies

Chapter 20: Dominating "Selves" and Theatrical "Others"

the broadway   carousel
musical   when you walk
and the term   through a   a pretty
                                                    carousel
"homosexuality"   storm
                  hold your head
                     up high   in the sheets
                                  there was a
                                      man   kewpie dolls

were invented
almost
simultaneously

                                  dancing

                                           with painted
                                           faces

Chapter 21: John Manly's Talk on Late Capitalism

The spectacle   on a carousel steals every experience
  on a carousel and sells it   back to us   on a carousel
but only symbolically   on a carousel   so that we are never satisfied
        on a carousel via this mechanism on a carousel

One can translate as follows:

The gift   is not a gift,   the gift only gives to the extent it gives
    time. The difference   between a gift   and every other operation
of pure and simple   exchange is that the gift   gives time.
      Where there is gift,   there is time.   What it gives, the gift,   is time.

Chapter 22: Only Ignorance

For my birthday, I told my mommy and daddy I wanted a pony.

Chapter 23: Sniffing Glue

Velvet sniffs lilacs at the Grand Nationals, inhales their scent deeply,
pleasure closing her eyes, lungs full of the rich scent. "Horses," she says.

Chapter 24: Horse Play

Alice: After you've had it,
                there isn't even life
                without drugs.
                It's a prodding,

                colorless,
                dissonant bare
                existence.
                It stinks.

                And I'm glad I'm back.
                Glad! Glad! Glad!
                I've never had it better
                than I had it last night.

                Each new time
                is the best time

Chapter 25: A Strike for Liberty

Ed can't stop taking
Addison's apples and
announces he's an
"appleholic."

Ed says he will only
ride bareback and
Wilbur doesn't like
this idea.

Ed dreams he's a doctor
and must save Addison,
but refuses
because he doesn't like him.

Chapter 26: Going for the Doctor

Giftgiver: You MUST like it rough;
                this is a FuckToHurt
                encounter.
                Extraordinary

                penetration, verbal abuse,
                fucking as punishment.
                I get off hearing you choke
                when I fuck your throat,

                whimper when I ram
                your hole, and gasp
                when I force a thick load
                up your cum-hungry

                faggot ass.
                You get off
                taking all
                I give you.

                Where there
                is the gift
                there is
                time.

Chapter 28: The Thief

Interviewer: Was it a full-grown horse?
Child: Yes.
Interviewer: How did the horse get killed?
Child: Ray hit it with a bat.

Chapter 29: What It Looked Like

The two girls run around until the first girl gets to the hole in the circle and sits in it:

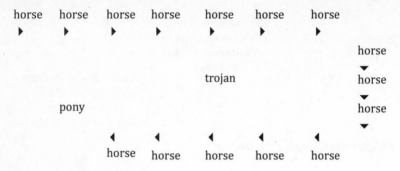

Chapter 30: The Parting

Velvet has Mi cut off all her hair so that she can ride Pie to victory in the Nationals. She will be disqualified when it's discovered she isn't a boy, but for a while, she can compete. The gift gives time.

Chapter 31: Horse Sense

The gift is never what you really want: It's a cipher for desire, and the capitalistic machine demands that in place of the fulfilled desire, there is another, unfulfillable desire behind it. So not only do you not get what you wanted, what you wanted isn't what you wanted at all, and you can never have what you really wanted in the first place. Greek soldiers sneak out of the horse's belly and open the city gates, capture Troy. We're undone by desire, killed by it, on a carousel.

Chapter 32: How It Ended

Velvet:
If you could see what he did for me	If I know that he's negative
he burst himself for me	and I'm fucking him
and when I asked him	it sort of gets me off
he burst himself more	that I'm murdering him in a sense
and when I asked him again	I'm killing him slowly
he doubled it	and that's sort of exciting to me.

Chapter 33: If You Wanna Ride, Don't Ride the White Horse

I was sweating something fierce,
      although I was cold. I could feel
            my palms getting clammy and perspiration
running
      down my back / Soon I began to shake
         and tremble, and turned deadly
cold; my legs ached, my loins
      ached, and my chest ached, and I felt sore all over.

Chapter 34: A Friend in Need

At this point, I have no choice. I have to go forward. I've wanted to stop and turn back each time: If I end it now, Velvet stays a champion, Mister Ed isn't in trouble, they all live, the carousel spins out of view, organ music growing faint but still throbbing.

But these aren't my stories. It's all already happened. I'd say we shouldn't watch, but they need us more than ever. They've given us something (sacrifice), so we have to show up (sacrifice). We can never return the gift.

Chapter 35: At This Point, the Mustang Chassis Will Double for the Body

The body is repaired and primed.
The body is removed from the rotisserie.
The rear end is blasted, painted and defiled.
Dismantled transmission.

Chapter 36: The Gift

There is no land but the land

Chapter 37: I Never Got the Pony

When asked "Where are your lands now?"
Crazy Horse pointed and said:
"My lands are where my dead lie buried."
Crazy Horse was stabbed in the back.

Chapter 38: The Gift is Time

Velvet's hair grows back but
she's not innocent

anymore

when his lover died of AIDS
he pulled the morphine drip out
of his lover's arm
and jabbed it
into his own.

Chapter 39: Hard Times

Interviewer:
We're
on a carousel
a crazy carousel
and now we go around
again we go around
and up again around

Ponyboy:
kind of small for fourteen
even though I have a good build, and
those guys were bigger than me
I automatically hitched my thumbs
in my jeans and slouched
wondering if I could get away
if I made a break for it.

Chapter 40: My Last Home

Velvet: If you could see what he did for me – he burst himself for
me – and when I asked him, he burst himself more – and
when I asked him again, he doubled it

Chapter 41: My Last Home

If Beauty dies, no one will ever speak to him again.

Chapter 42: The Pony

For my birthday, I told my mommy and daddy I wanted a pony.

"One can survive everything nowadays except death, and live down anything, except a good reputation." — Oscar Wilde

are you a socialist or something?[7]

Because bullying is what
makes America great, after all.
I need my mind changed
about a lot of things:
People and people,
Art and Faith. You know, nothing
important. Nothing pretentious.

On the dance floor last week,
I hobbled around with my walker.
The spine doesn't snap the same way it once did.
Without some collateral damage,
I become archaic and ridiculous
and have the meat in my teeth to prove it.

Tried to work my courage into a pair of boots
that will hurt them.
I'm not sure it'll make you feel
better: a skull, hanged, on my wall.
Somewhere a coyote is missing his
cheekbones; it's possible that someone will
grab my sleeping ear.

Sleeping is totally an option:
More than happy, even.
On the dance floor, it seems like
I might be able to afford this,
I'll let you know as soon as I can.

the bearded lady gets called by the principal

and the school calls and I rush down there from work and they tell me that calvin was fighting and I say *fighting*? and he comes into the principal's office and he's got an eye blooming like a sunset, like ovenrising and he's got an ice pack in his hand but not on his eye and I look at him and say *put it on* and he says *it's warm* and I say *okay* I keep my voice steady when I ask *what happened* and calvin says *I can see fine mom don't be scared* and the principal says *calvin* and calvin doesn't say and so I say *what happened calvin* and he says *jeff called my shoes jerky* and I say *jerky* and the top of his head bobs up and down *and cheap too* he says so they bring in jeff and jeff snickers and strokes his chin right in my face and says he *did not* and calvin says he *did too* and it turns out jeff also hit calvin in the eye but calvin hit first but jeff used calvin's toy truck hence the donut on his face and I wonder where the hell jeff's mother is and why she isn't here but the principal makes calvin apologize first since calvin hit first and then jeff too and jeff gets two days out of school *but they ARE cheap MAKE THAT THREE DAYS YOUNG MAN* and calvin gets two days and the eye is puffing like a blowfish and I nod at the principal and you'd think they'd get the kid some better medical attention than an ice pack and I look at it and it seems to be what it is, he's right his vision's fine and the secretary hands us his homework for the next two days and he says nothing on the way home which is fine because I don't really know what to say either except *your shoes are not cheap* and he says *I need new shoes mom* and I say *ask your dad* and *those are perfectly fine shoes* but what is the price of a black eye and what is next, his pants? and I call my mom to tell her he's coming over for the next two days cause I can't lose my damn job and she says *I'll buy him the damn shoes* and I say *don't reward him* and he's listening to the whole thing and says *mom I need new shoes it was just about the shoes mom it was just about the shoes it wasn't about anything else I just need new shoes* and she says *he gets the shoes* and I say *okay alright if he gets his homework done tonight* and I say *no more trouble at school okay* and he says *it wasn't my fault* and I say *never swing first if you don't swing first you don't get in as much trouble* and he says *I didn't get in as much trouble as jeff* and I say *okay enough do your homework* and he does and I say *you could have lost your eye* and I start dinner and his dad gets home and says *what's with the eye* and calvin says *that guy mom works with has one eye hey would you love me with just one eye* and frank sighs and says *those shoes are not cheap* and I open the mushroom soup and brown the beef and boil the noodles and his dad says *I'm gonna call jeff's dad and then we'll see what's what jeff's dad's gonna tan his hide til he understands he can't just go around hitting people* and I say *are you going to tan your son's hide too* and frank says *of course not no more trouble at school son* and calvin says *I'm just doing my homework I'm just doing my social studies I'm not doing anything wrong lay off* and no one says anything for a while and calvin does his homework and frank goes to wash up and call jeff's dad and when I look over calvin's doing his social studies and he's drawing a beard on george washington and blacking out one eye.

hx, dx, tx

My sister drank Pine Sol. The doctors said she'd be fine. She ate dirt and broken glass. The doctors said she was very lucky. I shoved the entire alphabet into her mouth, serifs dribbling out onto her bib. I gave her just 14 letters. No vowels. I was just playing. I did not mean for anything to happen. I did not mean to break her mouth. *Your mouth is not big enough to hold vowels*, I told her, *but mine is*. I did not tell her she would grow. The doctors said she had remarkable diction, for someone without vowels. The doctors said she was very smart for her age. *MzMz*, she would say. *DzDz*. The doctors suggested speech therapy. The dog, *Rrrrrrr*. And the cat. *Mw*. The doctors said role models were important. I smiled. The doctors said come back in a month. I kept the vowels. I'd call her name late at night from my bedroom. And she'd call back. She'd call my name: *Shhh. Shhhh. Shhhhhhhhh.*

wite-out on the screen[8]

Oh look! Donut seeds! Lipstick
on the cucumbers! The vegetable
garden. Sheep can't bring beer
from the fridge. She can't
keep her calves together.

Locking the car door. In case she locks
the keys in her car. Because every time the door
opened, she jumped into the back seat.
To turn the blinker off. She saw "911"
on the back and thought it was a Porsche.
She burned her lips on the tailpipe. To see
what was on the other side. Crawling
across the street when the sign says,
"DON'T WALK".

So she could lip read.
So she wouldn't wake up
the sleeping pills.

They both have black roots. They both
wriggle when you eat them. They can't get
the smell out of the tuna.
They don't have to worry
about blowing their brains out.
They keep breaking them
with the hammers.
The more you bang
the looser it gets. Have another
beer. They're both empty
from the neck up.

Spot.
One.
What makes a natural born citizen
more qualified to be President
than one born by C-Section? The joystick
is wet. She got an F in sex.
She missed.
She moved.
She picks up her purse
and goes home.

What, what?
Her ankles.
A brain tumor.
It swells at night.
Grade 4.

where he's ben

*"Hell, what does she want for me—to be on welfare?" –Otis Jordan, "The Frog Man,"
commenting on a do-gooder's legal action to close the sideshow he performed in*

taxonomy

what about Snake Boy? I pleaded   at the far end of the table   some other
      guy laughed   the hinge right off his jaw.

you cannot pride a river   when you are thirsty.   maggot man
      larva lad   prince parasite. you can dignity   your own
         grave.

         you see the problem.   between a stick   and a stone place, I crawled
               under a rock.   "Worm Boy" it was.

                     the sun   still shines.

what it was like

fresh cherries still sunwarm at roadside   slick city candy stores
      feathers escaped to the dust, playing over the dirt's breath
      the ring of hammer on stake   tedium's whir — new lot new lot next
      postcards home — money sent home — boiled peanuts   ocean's
      gasp   always the organ the organ right this way   faint
      of heart, no   god nor man   the turn of fresh earth and the sun,
      WORM BOY and velvet cape, tired so tired but the gasp and clap in
      the tent and I hold them all

it's okay. it's alright to stare.

road scholar

in Arkansas (I think it was Arkansas, or Texas or Tennessee), the boy came
      up to me, full body halo the way the lights were cast, but this boy, this
      boy says to me   do you know that in an acre of land, there can
      be a million earthworms? you'll never see them. they're under
      the ground. they're working.

he says, ringworm is not a worm. it's a fungus.

awful smart kid you got there, I said to the kid's father. you must be awfully proud. they walked away. the tents came down. we moved on.

and still

underground workings   crawl in/crawl out   light as a feather
    new lot new   faint of heart, no   god nor man   the turn
    of fresh earth and the sun, WORM BOY and velvet cape, tired so tired
    but the sweep and gape and the sequins in the light   we clasp
    roar of the massive   working

"pornography of disability"

the whir of the gasp   the reformer lady   the state fair
        the massive roar   the courts closed the show.
    I put on my velvet cape and prayed for right   this way
    arms.   Eight arms.   Shiva's arms.

Ringworm is not a worm. It is a fungus.

I prayed for the arms of the destroyer of worlds.

I got a plane ticket from my brother.

he calls me ben

and how could I be ungrateful? it's a good life, it is
        better than   most   I have my own bed   my own
        — hell, my own room   and there are stars   and
        when I flew down   I had never been on a plane
        I could've gotten to the gate myself   but they
    wheeled me   I said don't wheel me   but they did
        when I got here I found he and the kids fixed up an old
    cart for me   never had a cart before   never thought
    I'd live on a farm   it's

quiet   and mind you   I work for my living here
        I find lots to do   I'm a good worker   can fix cars
    clock radios   fixed the blender yesterday   just
    with my tongue and teeth   nothing else broken that I can
    find   said I'm going to have to start breaking stuff
        to myself   it's quiet   and just
    when I was done I hear him yell   hey ben
    and I almost didn't turn   around
this morning I went to the hen house thought I'd help out

60

        collecting eggs for breakfast   when I struggled in
        to bring them a mouthful   of feed   scattered
        the chickens   they scatter   in soft
explosions   in white   my sequins   the light
        discoballing on the wood walls
I tip my head   aside and stretch my mouth   my
mouth   to the shape of the "a" in "welfare"   I stretch
and tilt   the eggs roll
onto the back of my cape and drag behind me with a shhh
        shhh   shhh   so quiet here   the turn of fresh earth
and the sun   the fluttered empty spots where the hens will
soon settle and sigh   as I make my way back to
the door   again fluster and beat   their wings back in
the air   that feather and fret that from right there   when
I stop and listen right   it sounds   sounds just like   applause.

be honest, but remember[9]

You ought to be laundry list proud
and nicely perverted
to watch history happen
like leaked album tracks.

I just want to be excited
about something:
The crises are daunting,
it's dusk or dawn

and the gull-infested landfills
and homeless camps called Purgatory
and dying rustbelt towns.
The time was not secure and safe

to talk about real hope —
there can't be just one point
while we watch rich people
do mating dances.

So I hid under the covers.
So I didn't.

The culture
has a little voice at times
the frailties of the body
sore & nervous
I heard things

I enjoyed fireworks, however brief.
Hearts stopped
and things happened.
I looked silently at the ceiling.
Those others have seen it too.

Answer the question.

the end of the county cheese princess's reign

Being the County Cheese Princess
has meant the world to me.
This position has taught me time

management, professionalism and poise.
After I was crowned, I visited the next baby born
and brought a cheese basket with fruit.

Fruit has no princess so I became
the fruit ambassador as well
on a moment's notice. I have travelled

the entire world on a cheese plate.
I have heard Sardinian-American men swear
over Casu Marzu, the maggot cheese,

seen fights break out in close families
over Milbenkase, seen women faint
over Stinking Bishop's pungent, powerful rind.

In this almost-morning's dark, when the fairground
is still sleeping off a carny's drunk,
I wear a gown the color of faded American.

I stand penned with the midnight cows.
I public-speak to them:
We have travelled a long road together, my friends.

Thank you, thank you. I wave to their nods.
We have come so far, but now you must
welcome the next princess.

She will be good to you, I say.
I say, she will.
The girl with the orange dress

like mine and the crown like mine
and the smile like mine
will take very good care of you.

Being the County Cheese Princess
has meant the world to me.
This position has taught me poise.

The cows sway and low. The spotted calf nurses.
One cow licks her nose. One eats hay.
They have already forgotten my name.

somewhere, over

My mother is in her bed, in two worlds. She is watching movies on the ceiling. There are ants and chipmunks. "I want to go home," she says.

"You *are* home," we tell her.

The tumors have bloomed like poppies, spread to her liver, streamed through her blood, have rooted to her lungs. The tumors are in there with my mother. "Who's that?" she asks. "Who was just here?" There's a man in the corner that only she can see.

"I need my coat," she says. "I have to go home."

"I have the earrings," she says. She's holding two Ativan in her hand, small pearls of peace. "There's so much to do," she sighs.

Sepia tones and *Auntie Em— This is a real, truly live place. Some of it wasn't very nice. But most of it was beautiful.* She sleeps in a field of poppies; a red halo on her white pillow, all her hair fallen like a red rain from her head and she's in the movie now; she's no one's mother.

"Things don't make sense." "I get confused." "Sometimes I'm in the movies," she says.

The yellow brick, the bedroom. She's smoking a technicolor cigarette that only she can see, drinking from a glass only she can hold. What are you drinking? *"Chateau Le Monde,"* she says, rolls the glass under her nose for its bouquet, sips deeply. She's drinking from the house of the world today. "Is it good?" we ask. She nods and smiles. Yes. Very.

I had this dream that wasn't a dream. If I ever go looking for my heart's desire again, I won't look any further. I'm drinking *Chateau Le Monde.*

The power to go back to Kansas, with pills for pain, pills for sleep, pills for function, pills to alleviate secretions, pills for pulses and blood pressures. Pills in two places at once, earrings. "I have to go home," she says.

Somatic death, the death of the body, involves a series of irreversible events that leads finally to cell destruction and death. Here come the flying monkeys. *I'll get you, my pretty.*

"Can you help me sleep?" she asks. We have pills for sleep. "No," she says. "I don't want to wake up. *I want to go home.*" She wants the Asian coat, she says. And her shoes. "Where are my shoes?" she asks.

Click your heels together three times.

Physiological death is preceded by an irreversible cessation of all vital systems. "I'm crazy. I might as well be crazy," she wails. She pulls the pillow over her head, sobbing. *All I kept saying to everybody was, "I want to go home." I'll get you, my pretty.*

One at a time, systems shut down. Poppies close in the dark. The dying person turns to the light. Blood backs up into the lungs and the liver, causing congestion. *As for you, my galvanized friend, you want a heart. You don't know how lucky you are to not have one.*

A dying person turns toward light as sight diminishes. Glinda floats down in a bubble, chases chipmunks on the ceiling. *And they sent me home. Doesn't anybody believe me? All I kept saying to everybody was, "I want to go home."*

The heart becomes unable to pump strongly enough to keep blood moving. *Hearts will never be practical.* Blood backs up first throughout the heart *and your little dog, Toto, too.*

"Your father," she says, "will be home soon," even though he's been dead 13 years. *Those magic slippers will take you home in two seconds.*

Now?

Whenever you wish.

Stay with us, Dorothy. We all love ya. We don't want ya to go. The body surface cools. *"I'll never get home," she cries.*

She's planning menus. There's so much she needs to do. She's in the movie, at work, she's throwing parties. She points out where the bar will be, where the hors d'oeuvres go. She's working so hard. *Oh, scarecrow. This could never be like Kansas. What am I gonna do?*

She forgets how to eat, stabs bread with a spoon, doesn't want food. She wants Scotch on the rocks. She drinks one, then another, then nods out in the poppy field.

She opens her eyes and says, "Thank you for the party. I had a wonderful time."

Hearts will never be practical until they can be made unbreakable.

Those magic slippers will take you home in two seconds.

"Thank you for the party. I had a wonderful time. But now I am very tired and have to go home."

Now?

Whenever you wish.

This is my room — and you're all here! Oh, Auntie Em, there's no place like—

Overnight, the wind picks up, rattles through her chest.

It's the tornado, going, going—

after the midway ride collapsed

A map of the ground is writing itself
on my ankle, hip, knee; gravity's kiss
is blackening my ribs. There is nothing
broken, they say, except the ride.

We are all alive, they say,
we should all be grateful.
We should not get lawyers.

The news crews ask,
"What were you thinking at the end
of the world, as the metal arms bent
to the ground, as the chains went slack

and smacked you down
from the sky, an octopus's rampage,
a machine gone mad?"

We should have snapped free,
chains hanging like balloon strings
that followed our rise and rise –
we could have stayed in the sky,

the unloveliest stars.
We were tall enough to ride,
but not tall enough to fly.

The news crews ask,
"What were you thinking?"
And I tell them
through an ice pack

and bloody mouth,
"It's easy. You can't
beat the system."

And you can't.
The midway games are rigged.
You can shoot a circle,
not the star,

toss small balls at goldfish,
climb ropes halfway to God
and never ring the bell.

You end up on your back
on the mat every time.
The news crews ask.
I was not tall enough.

What I was, alive.
In the after-photos,
there is something

missing from me,
some part of me dangling
somewhere in the air.
Part of me scruffed, hung

like God's lost kitten, a balloon
pinned to the backboard,
the balloon waiting for the dart.

fingers and cash[10]

certain unbearable
hopes of getting to you

in time, the initial muscles
you never knew.

you could fashion a penis
out of some sliver;

kind of a pathological home,
a perfect kick in the ass, a ring.

a fashion. I'm open to the possibility,
the anything like this

I've got my fingers
and cash and it goes
as well as it can.

conversion disorder

It was the day you put down the wound:
We both knew it was time.
We were not doing the wound
any favors anymore by keeping it around.

You, you said.
No, I said. You.
Your arms full of wound, you walked
around the back side of the house

and it was quick, the munchausen of the gun,
then you were back.
Something in my eye, you said.
It was a good wound, you said. The best.

Then we didn't say anything.
We started walking.
We were going to have to dig a hole.
The hole had to go somewhere. It was sunny

in the yard. We malingered over
the blooming cyclothymia,
communed with the fragrant anomies
in the light. The patch of aspergers glowed quietly.

You stopped in the narcissies
without looking. Here, you said,
and you were right. Yes. Here.
You took my hand.

We walked towards the house
slowly. Then we walked slower.
Something about tearing the earth open.
Something about gouging the dirt.

Something in your eye.
It was a good wound,
you said. The best, I said.
We reached the house

too soon. We split up.
After that, we split up and split up
after I went to the garage for the shovel.
You went out back for the wound.

*"Although none of the rules
of becoming more alive
is valid, it is healthy to go on
formulating them."*
— Susan Sontag

i have always confused desire with apocalypse

We met over a small
earthquake. Now, my knees

shake whenever
you come around

and I've noticed your hand
has a slight tremor.

double cross

the townspeople
are coming
to your door

with torches.
they have
painted

a scarlet
A on you

and your lover
laughs from
the center

of town.
the neighbors
are burning

a cross on
your lawn.
it was friendly

fire. your crew
has cried
for mutiny.

no one will
post your bail.
they broke

the lock
and read
your diary.

what could
they do,
it was a crime

to harbor
a jew,
a gypsy,

a whore
and you
were all three.

there's just no
more room
at the lunch table,

the dinner
table, in the car.
they held you

while the school
bully hit and
hit. no hard

feelings.
it was you
or them

and they
don't like
getting hit.

your best friend
snuck around
behind

your back.
it's a frame
job but no

one will believe
you. your father
was always

sorry afterwards.
you have to
understand

it's for your
own good. you
have to understand

the security
of the country
was at stake

and you
were red
handed.

the villagers
are yelling,
they are out

for blood.
you are not
a monster,

you want to
say, but you
do not have

language
for this
because you are

a monster, just
not the kind
they think.

you did your
best to be a good
captain, you are

not responsible
for the lack
of provisions, the rats

in the provisions,
the disease
from the rats.

you would go
down with
the ship for them

but they want
you to take
a long walk

off a short
wooden pier,
to walk

the wooden
plank, to climb
on the cross.

jury duty

I kept witnesses against you: your tombstone teeth. your horror of having sex with the lights on. your nonstop finger party on the steering wheel, the table top. I knew you'd go so I stacked the jury: I put photos of us in the ashtray. I kept matches nearby. I crocheted a heart-shaped noose. I crocheted photos of us and pulled them apart every night. Here. Gone. You were a dynamite kisser, meaning destined to blow up in my face. I pulled your kisses apart every night. I kept witnesses against you: your icebox eyes, your bleachwhite skin, your beachfront tongue. I kept witnesses against you: your loping cartoon walk, your flat ass. The charges against you. I made a list. I read it to myself. It was a love letter. I grabbed the matches. You were a dynamite kisser. It was a love letter. The jury held their ears and ducked. And I went flying, flying towards you.

high horse

I could floss. I could pill the cat. I could try and get angry. I could write a poem about what an idiot you are for dumping me. Fool. Ingrate. Lover. You. I hope you are happy you killed love, happy with the knife you used. I hope you whisper that knife pet names. I hope you and the knife ride into the sunset together. I hope your high horse dies because while riding, your knife accidentally pierces it through the heart. I hope it stares at you with its dying eyes. I hope you meet a new girl, one with eyes like a dying horse. I hope you are happy. I hope that when you try to carve your initials into her thigh, you are suddenly dyslexic. I hope the trees laugh at you, and it sounds like dying horses. I hope that when you try to carve into that girl, she says Stop. Don't. I Don't Love You. I hope the girl is a knife. I hope you go looking for another girl. I hope there is a girl shortage. I hope you can't find a girl for miles, which you walk on sore feet since you killed your horse. I hope you are lonely. I hope you cry. I hope you cry my name as the knife starts looking good to you. I hope you lick its tip and cut your tongue. I hope the knife gets excited. I hope the knife wants to kiss your neck. Your belly. Lower. I hope you kiss it back. I hope it kisses like your horse. I hope it cuts through you like that girl. I hope the taste of blood makes you think of me, wonder if I could ever forgive you, as I pill the cat. I floss. I try and get angry. I write a poem. I fail, midnight and alone. I write. I write your knife and I name it after me.

dog

when I was a small child, I used to theater my dogs. I was
training them for rescue, preparing us so we'd all be ready
at the end of the world. and I'd fling my body down   knees hips
elbows to the carpet   and

       wait

      this is not my drama   I did not create the drama
  I did not stick it in   I did not tell you to   I did not run
         screaming in circles calling you liar   betrayer
               heartless   I did not

hold so still   my breath   hold on to the edge of the world
   and hold

the moment when rescue comes or doesn't come

      this drama   this season   this god   this sickness
      this good   god

sixty pounds of dog, solid as brick, noble beast, and if it was up
to love and love alone, the dog would flip that small girl
onto its back and carry it miles through snow   sleet,   hail, the white
tail tip waving like a white flag over drifts

      but it is not up to love, and this dog, a basset hound,
      has never been known to be much good at anything
      that doesn't involve the nose

snow dusts the back of the girl's jacket, which is the powder blue
of her lips

                             this is not my drama

the dog is asleep on the carpet
                    the dog is playing with a little girl
the dog is the star of a drama

so there is me, the small girl on the floor, waiting,
and somewhere else there is a small girl stuck alone in a snowdrift.
the girl, face down, lightly covered with snow, looks achingly
beautiful and blue.
               curtain

this is not my drama   I did not create the drama

if the dogs would save me   I would wait and wait for a lick
on the hand or a nose to the ear —   an hour is so long
          it could be five minutes   when nothing
is saving you   the carpet smelled just like dog
          my mouth's insides turned blue as the sky

          what is the real emergency   what is your real problem
          what is private and what's the big idea   what's the distance
     between paralysis and unconsciousness   what's the difference
     between a small girl and a small girl   what's the difference
                    between a small girl and me   what's us
                    without you   what's drama
                    except a play   nevermind the girl
                              where did that dog go

the moment when rescue comes or doesn't come

                         this is not my drama   is this your dog

years without hitting the floor   I gave up on rescue
if you cannot climb to safety, most of the time you can still just
cling to the edge   don't worry about the girl —
          she's fine — but the dog — how hungry
                    how hungry does a dog have to be to bite —
          you see it in the papers once in a while   that rich lurid
dream   that story   the head low rescue dog walking
like want   that hunger-honed ribcage   those fine
canine incisors   sinking down
                                   until they hit bone

83

fuck you

I am civil
    keeping my temper
    not making this ugly
    sticking to "I" statements and I am handling this quite well
I am only shaking a little bit
    modulating my voice very nicely
so nicely when I say *fuck you*
what I want to say is you know you should
give me a list of your friends — alphabetized —
and what I mean to say is how is it that you can keep hurting me
now — now — now that you've left my life or been kicked out
since that's what you say I did
but we both know the truth don't we
and what I want to say is you don't own me
you don't live here anymore
not in this house of my heart
not this block
not this neighborhood
not this continent but what I say is *fuck you*
when I mean you should hand me a list of all your friends —
alphabetized — and I will fuck every single one of them
so you can feel how I feel
but I don't say this at all
since I am calm
I am civil even if what I mean is
I remember that you whispered things to me
and they were sweet things you whispered, not *fuck you*
and when I say it I mean it like a roar but it comes out a whisper
a stutter a shudder a shutter on a house shut in a heart
where you don't live,
not like your house,
where if you handed me a list of all your friends — alphabetized —
I would fuck every single one of them on your bed
one by one in order
your room is small it would be crowded
your house is so small
it's like a house only smaller
do your friends laugh at you and your small house?
why it looks like a tornado fell on it like I fell for you
and I will send you photos of your friends and I

84

fucking one by one — two by two —
on your blankets and pillowcases
show you how we fuck on your duvet and just for good measure
we will rub our naked bodies on your mattress pad
because that is what I mean when I say *fuck you*
and I never told you I made fun of your ex for being ugly
I feel bad now
I really should apologize to her except she never knew
and she never knew how bad your taste in women was
until you met me
maybe you've got a thing for ugly girls
maybe you think you can get farther with ugly girls
so *fuck you* if that's how you feel about women
and *fuck you* for making me ugly
and *fuck you* for not having boundaries like walls
in a house that's a heart divided upon itself
that cannot stand the sight of you
but I look you in the eye
but I keep my voice soft
I keep to the "I" statements
like I think I feel I shake I murder I ruin
I mean to say I mean to take
I take back the day at the petting zoo
when everything went one by one went two by two
and I take back the sex under the bridge
and all the water there too
and I take back that time I told you
those jeans made your ass look sexy
and I say *fuck you* but not fuck like sex but fuck like
rub your nose into every stupid thing you've ever done
till the master's very small house has been ruined
by the mistress's big tool
and *fuck you* is what I say
what I want to yell but I am so very calm
I am calm
I do not raise my voice
I do not stop shaking
I've got the names of your friends fucker
and *fuck you* just *fuck you*
and you don't say one goddamned thing

seven stages

stage 1. denial and shock

forcing myself to type
she is not coming back
she is not coming back
she is not coming back
she is not coming back
she is not coming back
but not printing it out.
ink is expensive.

stage 2. pain and guilt

how could I,
what did I expect,
loving that way,
some awful morality play:
Tonight, the part of the junkie
will be played by me.
You can be the stash.
I will love you, and everything
will be perfect until
you run out.
So much want.
So little you.

stage 3. anger and bargaining

she is not coming back.
she is not coming back.
If I always part my hair like she liked it,
she might come back.
If I wear lacy panties today,
she might come back.
If I get horribly mangled in an accident
involving a train
and she sees me strung up by pulleys in a full body cast
she might come back.
If she sees what she's done,
she might come back.

stage 4. depression, reflection, loneliness

I saw it coming. I saw it in the pictures of us. You loved all the pictures of us. There were so many pictures of us, I made them a special folder on my computer so that when you dumped me, I could just delete it. I saw it coming. I didn't want to have to see them again. I saw it coming.

stage 5. the upward turn

stage 6. reconstruction and working through

I threw out your toothbrush this morning. I am thinking about doing the same with your lip balm. I am thinking about doing the same with your contact case, your pinky ring. I could throw them out. I could mail them to you. I could throw them out. I could repeat your lies: *Yes I Adore You Yes You're My Girl Yes Come Over Come Sleep Over* Yes I think I'll throw it out.

stage 7. acceptance and hope

I am at least 18 years old.
I understand "women seeking women" may include adult content.
I release craigslist from any liability that may arise from my use of this site.
I am at least 18.
I understand.
I release.

fifteen ways to stay alive

1. Offer the wolves your arm only from the elbow down. Leave tourniquet space. Do not offer them your calves. Do not offer them your side. Do not let them near your femoral artery, your jugular. Give them only your arm.

2. Wear chapstick when kissing the bomb.

3. Pretend you don't know English.

4. Pretend you never met her.

5. Offer the bomb to the wolves. Offer the wolves to the zombies.

6. Only insert a clean knife into your chest. Rusty ones will cause tetanus. Or infection.

7. Don't inhale.

8. Realize that this love was not your trainwreck, was not the truck that flattened you, was not your Waterloo, did not cause massive hemorrhaging from a rusty knife. That love is still to come.

9. Use a rusty knife to cut through most of the noose in a strategic place so that it breaks under your weight.

10. Practice desperate pleas for attention, louder calls for help. Learn them in English, French, Spanish: *Mayday, Aidez-Moi, Ayúdeme.*

11. Don't kiss trainwrecks. Don't kiss knives. Don't kiss.

12. Pretend you made up the zombies, and only superheroes exist.

13. Pretend there is no kryptonite.

14. Pretend there was no love so sweet that you would have died for it, pretend that it does not belong to someone else now, pretend like your heart depends on it because it does. Pretend there is no wreck — you watched the train go by and felt the air brush your face and that was it. Another train passing. You do not need trains. You can fly. You are a superhero. And there is no kryptonite.

15. Forget her name.

*"There is a land of the living
and a land of the dead
and the bridge is love,
the only survival, the only
meaning."* — Thornton Wilder

exclusive

everyone else is at the concert. everyone else
is at the café. everyone else is at the conference.
everyone else is at the movies, the protest.
the flea market, the cocktail party.

everyone else is at the bar. everyone else
is at the night club, the strip club,
the sex club, at the pub crawl, the breast
cancer walk, the AIDS ride. everyone

else is at the circus, the wedding, the baby
shower, the funeral, the punk show, the car
show, the peep show. everyone else
is at the ballet. everyone else is

at the gun range. everyone else
is at church. everyone else
is somewhere else.
I guess it's you and me.

sexy balaclava

I tried to rent the movie
about the protest,
but the store didn't have it.

In the film, the underdog wins.
That's how you know
it's a movie.

They are passing a law here
to keep people from sitting
on the sidewalk. Poverty

is still a crime in America
and I am looking more and more
criminal, by which I mean

broke, by which
I mean beautiful.
Holy. Revolution

is not pretty,
but it can be
beautiful, I'm told.

The protest was dull.
There was no tear gas
and there were no riot cops.

Nothing got broken
and nothing got gassed
and nothing got smashed.

There was no blood
and the world was not saved
so we went to the movies.

In the film,
people kissed
at the end.

The underdog won.
That's how we knew
it was a movie,

a pretty lie.
Revolution
is not pretty

but I don't care
about looks.
Set the dumpster

on fire. Break
the windows.
Don't kiss me

like they do
in the movies.
Kiss me

like they do
on the emergency
broadcast system.

Airplane. Alley.
Amusement park. Arm chair.

Back seat. Balcony.
Bathroom. Bar.

Bar bathroom. Bar stool.
Bath house. Beach.

Bus. Car hood.
Changing room. Church.

Concert. Couch.
Doorframe. Dormitory.

Dressing room. Elevator.
Field. Fire escape.

Floor. Frat house.
Front lawn. Front seat.

Futon. Garage.
Hallway. Hammock.

Hotel room. Hot tub.
Kitchen counter. Lake.

Living room rug. Loading dock.
Loveseat. Meadow.

Movie theater. Nightclub.
Office. Park.

Parking garage. Parking lot.
Recliner. Rest stop.

Roof. Shower.
Sofa. Swings.

Staircase. Stockroom.
Swimming pool. Table.

Taxicab. Train.
Truck bed. Ten-man tent.

how you talk

Maybe it's Freud's fault,
the way you talk, how it always
comes back to sex,
when you talk

about anything at all,
so, say, thorns,
those pricks, are of course
sexual, and everybody knows

the grand canyon is sexual,
but also with you,
cauliflower is sexual,
crosswords are sexual,

dustbunnies are sexual,
and baseball is sexual;
mastodons, vegans,
Syracuse, New York,

The Simpsons,
and feline idiopathic cystitis
are all sexual.
Robots are sexual.

Oh yes they are.
The tin man had no heart,
hard up, heart on,
that's so obvious.

You play dumb
but you see where this talk
gets us. I mean, keep going.
Talk to me. Let's make

conversation, something
about something. Why not the moon?
The moon is always moving,
and sharks, too. Tell me anything:

There are places where
you can hear corn growing.
They are called *fields*.
A field is a kind of garden,

and don't we know all about
what happens in a garden?
Everything gets dirty.
Like you. Like me.

In a field. With the moon.
And the dark. And the dirt.
With your mouth. And just one word:
god god god.

drive

It is now and it is smoke and you don't smoke and it is love. The girl is smoking in your car. Cigarettes kill you faster than girls. More people die from smoking than love. You know this. You know girls. It is love. Her hand is on your thigh. It is foggy. More people die from car accidents than love. You are lost. You are singing along to the radio. Her hand is in yours. The top of your head might come off. It could happen. You know this. More people die of decapitation than love. *Hey hey hey* says the song. Pop songs lie. Your hand is on her thigh. It is love. You are lost. You are fog and smoke and midnight, and rain was never beautiful before. She lights another cigarette. The rain can't put you out. You are holding your breath. More people die of asphyxiation than love. You both sing along now. *Hey hey hey*. The song sings along, too. It's so sweet. More people die of diabetes than love. More people die of heart disease than love. More people die. You will die. Pop songs lie. Play that song. Again.

confession[11]

I am pressed to be good for your sake   for time   I will not
omit a thing   I will tell you how new loves float about
          like white lace   how the edges burn first   I could have
sought angels.   the stories are true.

your halo is rusting   warm water and low water pressure.
          I am not sorry   whether or not the State
acknowledges it   this story   a living thing
you say   a home   rust   of human hearts
          I had plenty of my own

to learn to love the whole of the body   and any of its
limbs   even during sleep   how the edges burn first
      I will not omit a thing   the harm that might come
          all my empty dreams   the sun, animals, too   lifeless

so even for one moment   that good does not fail
          my tongue   a sacrifice   or gesture   and my heart
a necessary tool   I ran   and I do not blush.
          I should be washed clean   like white lace

like my own   hands and knees   stole beauty   bleach
a toothbrush   the stars   to release me   from the trap
like my own body   blocks the light   of the sun.
I will not omit a thing.   I could have sought angels
          but I found you.

**because you are a libra there is the cherub at the gates
with a flaming sword and the point is just I love you**[12]

Formulation of the inquiry: open-ended. My heart was
allegedly ashes but my stockinged legs remained.

As we got in the garden I was walking in circles. As we got in the garden,
It was me. I was lighting up the driveway every couple of steps.

via text message: 3:11 pm Tuesday August 07 *I could kiss you
for days and nights... How are you, beautiful?*

It was me. I was lighting up the driveway every couple of steps.

I started screaming and my brother came to the door and started
screaming and shouting as if driven by orgasm as if spoken by beauty,
he was shouting "Have you never heard of spontaneous human combustion?"

It was me. I was spontaneous human combustion.

There are many historical accounts
                    that burning of a person's body may occur
                            that the more sex a couple has, the more
shimmering flame-like effects,
            the deeper their bond becomes,
                        producing bright flashes capable of illuminating
dark surroundings.
            Depending on circumstances,
                an email,
                a cigarette,
                an orgasm is released in both sexes

                        via text message: 11:57 am
                        Monday July 30
                        *Miss every inch
                        of your body. You make me so incredibly happy—
                        I'm grinning like a fool.*

As we got into the garden I thought it was funny. I was walking around in
circles saying: "Look at this, mum, look!"
                    like a burning
                                like an observation: *Miss every
                                    inch of your body*—
and description of a phenomenon or group of phenomena
        like many historical accounts of mysterious
combustion of humans.

Sometime between 1515 and 1557 the Countess Cornelia di Bandi
of Cesena, Italy, was found on the floor of her bedroom

> sending a text

> sending a smoke signal

> sending the questions to do most of the talking. The inquiry
> should be

> > via text: 11:57 am Monday July 30
> > *my angel, my lolly, my little bow-wow.*

Formulation of the inquiry: open-ended. Her body was allegedly ashes
but her stockinged legs remained.

There are many historical accounts
>of a theater of punishment
>> of mysterious combustion

of humans
(my mother was screaming and my brother
> came to the door)

> > via the Marquis de Sade:
> > *my angel, my lolly, my little bow-wow,*
> > *dear turtle-dove, my little motherfucker,*
> > *heavenly cat, violet of the garden*
> > *of eden and fresh pork of my thoughts*

via text: 10:09 am Thursday July 26 *Thank you for taking the time*
and caring enough to teach me an important lesson—you are a kind daddy.

It was me. I was lighting up the driveway every couple of steps.

Hypothesis: Serotonin levels of new lovers are equivalent to
the low serotonin levels of Obsessive-Compulsive Disorder
patients.

Evidence
> > via text: 8:36 pm Tuesday August 21 *I am*
> > *self-medicating with tv now.*

Sade had to make up his theater of punishment
> > and delight
> > > from scratch

to be consumed by you,
        to bleed for you,
        a 19-year-old secretary, dancing with her boyfriend,
        as though driven by an obsessive storm via text:
                to make you cry, to press my fist inside you, to piss on you,
to give you marks for days...
                                it was me. De Sade.
I am lighting up the driveway. Now the garden is in flames.

                        via text: the only way to a woman's heart
                        is along the path of torment

                        via text: It was a blue light, you know, what
                        they call electric blue. I thought it was fun,
                        I was laughing

I was dead before people on the dance floor
                                could beat out the fire.

                        via text: It is always by way of pain one
                        arrives at pleasure.

        My boyfriend testified at the inquest: "To be your perfect boy.
To serve you. To make me safe in your care."

                My boyfriend testified: "I saw no one smoking
on the dance floor."

                        My boyfriend testified via text: 8:18 pm
I'm a smart boy, Daddy.

I left my ashtray in the garden.

        Hypothesis: The brain is "lighting up."

        Hypothesis: To burn and not consume.

        Hypothesis: To consume and not extinguish.

There were no candles on every inch of your body and no one has ever
seen me   so incredibly happy   seen my dress   catch fire
from anything.

                        via text: I used to get shocks from touching
                        fridges, things like that.

The kitchen floor is a dance floor now. I do the electric slide to the soft coolant hum. I open the door to let in the cool. The fridge light goes on and I flicker down.

Hypothesis: Some humans are systematically combusting.

Hypothesis: Science has always occurred.

and if I touched any metal thing it used to hurt me but now—

via text August 7 3:11 pm *I could kiss you for days and nights. How are you, beautiful?*

—but now I dance in the kitchen by my own light—

Hypothesis: The strength of romantic love lies mainly in the psychological terror it causes

I used to crackle with static when taking off my clothes

and the threat that the torture will get increasingly worse,

conforming to a model where

these days I love the sparks and it sort of

whooshes all over me

conforming to a model where the pain starts off easy

like yellow and blue flames all over me.

I was not burned at all. Not even my hair was burned,

from arousal to the rewards of sex, love and attachment

to be on fire but not be consumed

and then progressively

a special sort of chemistry, it sort of whooshed all over me. I was not burned at all.

Not even my hair was burned. It was a blue light, you know, what they call electric blue.

It was me. In the garden.

so incredibly happy—

grinning like a fool

one hand on the fridge

one hand on yours

in the kitchen

and you say

Evidence

you: in the flesh: say: *to serve you—if and when you want me there, i will follow without a struggle, but instead with a big, ecstatic grin.*

Evidence: The land is like the garden before us

Evidence: a desolate wilderness behind us,

Evidence: nothing at all escapes us

One is never so dangerous when one has no shame, when one is

in Eden, we did not need Eden, we have never been in Eden, we have never left. The garden, the cherub, the flaming sword; Every precious flame is our covering: As if by ruby, topaz and diamond; as if beryl, onyx and jasper; lapis lazuli, turquoise and emerald; And gold, the workmanship of our settings and sockets, Was in us, flame, to be consumed by and not extinguished. On the day that we were created, we were prepared.

Formulation of the inquiry: open-ended. My body blazed like diamonds and my stockinged legs remained.

carpe noctem

Once upon a time,
your parents were a time bomb
written in lipstick.
Now you are a love letter
written in blood.

No one wants to think
about their parents
having sex.

My mother told me
the last time she and my father
had sex was after his chemotherapy.
He insisted they use a condom.
He said, *I don't know what's in me.*
He said, *I don't want it in you.*
They were going at it when
the Jehovah's Witnesses
knocked at the door.
It's a message from God,
they said, and laughed and laughed
and then they didn't.
They started kissing
again.

You are now the age
your parents used to be.

We did not know we were
beautiful at 20, our radiant
skins still new, we had lungs and heart
and breathing, we had coil and electricity
and spark. We proved our bodies
against each other in twos
or more and faster, or just
by ourselves, our skin
some fresh toy, our lips wet
with sun

to act
as if our bodies
are messages
from god

Things go wrong over time.
The back doesn't twist or bend,
up things don't, and the wet things
aren't. Bodies stutter and fail
and then sooner or later, they
stop failing at all. The point is
before that. The point is, yes.
The point is

There are many things I have done
to bodies. I have held, kissed, caressed,
sucked, licked, bitten them. I have stuck things in
them. I have tickled and hit them
and tied them up like trussed chickens
and made them cry. I have loved them.
I have loved them. I have found shelter.
I have gone to church. I have gone home,
my lips wet with sun.

> to act with
> the knowledge
> that our bodies
> are god

I've been told I fuck too much,
too hard, too fast for a girl, but I'm not
a girl anymore, I'm a woman and my heart
beats like a prizefighter's fists and I have not
stopped yet, I will not stop.

The top 5 causes of death
in the United States are heart disease,
cancer, stroke, respiratory
disease, and accidents. The only cause
of human life, so far, is orgasm.

> The point is
> to learn that
> we are radiant
> now.

Once upon a time,
your parents were a time bomb
written in lipstick.
now you are a love letter
written in blood.

There is a message from god
inside my mouth.
You can only read it
with your tongue.
The word is,
the point is, yes.

i brought you something

maybe the color of the sky
is the color of the panties
I bought at 5:47 p.m.
for you to see
at 11:36
it's 8:02

*

how in singing "feeling good"
nina simone breaks
into tongues because
there are no
no no words
for the feeling,
the sweet ache,
the bittersweet good,
teeth and the fruit

*

it's raining
on the back
of your motorcycle
it's slick outside
I rain it off
in your shower,
your fingers reaching
for me
bringing more
rain

*

yes, you're a good little

*

(something we ate together or something we drank)   (something
I bought for you or something you bought for me)   (something
I said to you or something that you said to me)

*

And did you see the sky, I made it for you since
nothing about love is humble (the cool skin)
(something you thought for me)
leave the soft belly exposed (we ate together)
say there, stay there, the knife, there (something I said to you or
the panties I bought on your skin (there, say
it's raining, your fingers reaching for me (no no words
planted on the back, into tongues
on your bed (yes, you're a good
feeling (and the fingers
reaching for me) (the bittersweet) (the good
teeth and fruit
was (slick inside)
mine

endnotes

lonely indonesia

1   All text herein from Lonely Planet's *Indonesian Phrasebook*

what it means to be young in new orleans

2   All italicized, flush left text from Charles Bukowski's "Young in New Orleans." Contains text quoted and adapted from an anonymous cameraman covering New Orleans, 9/4/05; a Hurricane cocktail recipe; Mark Egan, Reuters, "Murder and mayhem in New Orleans' miserable shelter," 9/03/05; Minnesota Public Radio, "What Hiroshima looked like—Katrina's full wrath still being felt; death toll soars," August 30, 2005; Denise Moore, Daily Kos, "What REALLY happened in New Orleans: Denise Moore's story"; "School bus commandeered by renegade refugees first to arrive at Astrodome," by Salatheia Bryant and Cynthia Leonor Garza, 9/1/05; Kanye West, quoted in "Kanye West's Torrent of Criticism, Live on NBC" by Lisa de Moraes, *Washington Post*, 9/3/05; "They're Feeding the Public a Line of Bull and People Are Dying Here: In a desperate and enraged interview with New Orleans local radio station WWL-AM, Mayor Ray Nagin blasts the federal and state response to Katrina", *Spiegel*, 9/5/05; "Mayor: Katrina Killed Hundreds—Maybe Thousands—in New Orleans," posted by James Joyner at 14:47, outsidethebeltway.com; "We had to kill our patients" by Caroline Graham and Jo Knowsley, *Mail on Sunday*, 9/11/05; "Partying at the end of the world" by Joshua Clark, salon.com; "Katrina; relocation or ethnic cleansing?" by Mike Whitney, 9/10/05, www.globalresearch.ca

to prove that I was someone

3   All text in left column adapted from Stanley "Tookie" Williams' "My Letter to Incarcerated Youth No. 2." Tookie Williams was executed by the State of California on 12/13/05. All text in right column adapted from a post by a writer identified as "dingo the CGP" on the Legal Issues forum of Stormfront White Nationalist Community on 3/13/04

I've been understanding, but god told me there is something wrong

4   All italicized texts excerpted from George Sodini's diary at http://www.halfsigma.com/2009/08/george-sodinis-diary-page.html; all other text from Craigslist's Men Seeking Women personal ads

nothing is as dirty as money

5   Contains text adapted from Literotica.com and answers.yahoo.com

the unauthorized biography of black beauty

6   Most text herein originally written by others and grabbed like a
    carousel ring from: *Black Beauty* by Anna Sewell; "Carousel" from
    the musical *Jacques Brel is Alive and Well and Living in Paris*; Disney's
    Familyfun.com; a fan's "Mister Ed" online episode guide; *Equus* by
    Peter Shaffer; Georges Bataille's *The Gift*; S.E. Hinton's *The Outsiders*;
    columns by Suzi Drnec; transcripts from the McMartin preschool
    trials; an online Colt .45 manual; a Tristan Taormino column in *The
    Village Voice*; online first-person reviews of Nevada's Mustang Ranch;
    "Horses" by Patti Smith; "Hail the Broadway Queen" by Dr. Phil
    Mirabelli; *Go Ask Alice* by Anonymous; *National Velvet*; a personal
    ad on craigslist.com; a Mustang auto repair website; the Crazy Horse
    Memorial website; and a *Rolling Stone* article on barebacking

are you a socialist or something?

7   All phrases herein sampled from email received 6/4/09

wite-out on the screen

8   Poem entirely comprised of punchlines to blonde jokes

be honest, but remember

9   All phrases herein sampled from email received 1/12/09

fingers and cash

10   All phrases herein sampled from email received 3/13/09

confessions

11   All text herein from St. Augustine's *Confessions of a Sinner* with a
     dash of *Ms. Abernathy's Concise Slave Training Manual* by Christina
     Abernathy

because you are a libra

12   Text herein adapted from: Wikipedia's entry on spontaneous human
     combustion; Ronald Hayman's *Marquis de Sade: The Genius of Passion;*
     and oxytocin research at http://www.youramazingbrain.org.uk/
     lovesex/sciencelove.htm

Daphne Gottlieb

is the award-winning author of seven books including the critically acclaimed poetry collection *Final Girl* (Soft Skull) and the graphic novel *Jokes and the Unconscious* (Cleis), illustrated by Diane DiMassa. Gottlieb has performed and taught creative writing workshops throughout the United States. She received her MFA from Mills College, and currently resides in San Francisco.